PYTHON CODING 2022 DATA ANALYSIS

5 WAYS TO LEARN PYTHON PROGRAMMING LANGUAGE - DATA ANALYSIS

SARA JACKLINE

Python Coding 2022: Data Analysis:

5 Ways To Learn Python Programming Language – Data Analysis

Introduction

On the off hazard which you are wishing to grasp programming and also you want to be a expert with the aid of using studying the necessities and building up a advanced seeing then you definitely ought to get the Python Book of programming language. This ee-e book is right for the ones those who want to self-educate with out deciding on themselves in a category for figuring out what writing laptop packages are.

The ee-e book has an adaptable content material which makes it easier for the man or woman to realize the nuts and bolts. A software program engineer can start with none training and end up a grasp with time with the help of this ee-e book. The those who want to get a respectable keep of what programming language is must get the Python books. Indeed, even a fledgling can get a respectable keep of the fundamentals of programming with this ee-e book because it covers all of the elements of the language pinnacle to bottom. All zones which are primary for a amateur to research were clarified.

The those who understand programming can likewise be profited with the aid of using this ee-e book as they could easy their abilties and alternate their thoughts. A tenderfoot could want to enjoy all of the substance but at the off hazard which you are an completed developer, you may likewise skirt the regions which you clearly know.

Aside from truly the "how-to" technique the ee-e book likewise consists of stunts and gainful coding methods that may be virtually green for the developer. With this ee-e book in a meeting, you may not want to enjoy specific books in order to realize the thoughts in subtleties. The ee-e book is cautious in itself. There isn't always downright content material withinside the ee-e book, it likewise consists of outlines, designs, and photo references for constructing up a advanced comprehension of the thoughts.

The ee-e book has exacting suggestions for the perusers. Customary simply as operational factors of view of writing laptop packages are with the aid of using all account now no longer the best topics which are secured, the ee-e book recalls upgrades simply as adjustments for those viewpoints.

It moreover includes guidelines for investigating and there are likewise notes closer to the end of each module.

Perusing the ee-e book is pleasant sufficient because it has were given all of the references that one may also require. Despite the reality that there are numerous programming books available withinside the marketplace but, there's one factor that may not alternate and it is the sample of perusing the Python ee-e book of programming. This ee-e book is certainly the unquestionable requirement for each one of these software program engineers who want to hold a few reference whilst programming. It isn't always truly implied for the apprentices but in addition, the maximum skilled software program engineers can require it as a form of attitude material.

Whatever you want may be something however hard to show upward and it'll become being an exceedingly superb guide for you.

Search for the ee-e book at the internet and purchase it currently to make it a few help in programming.

Learn Python Programming Language

Python is a programming language created with the aid of using Guido van Rossum. It is a powerfully composed language with enormous degree records systems. It is applied in diverse spots together with Google and Nasa.

Highlights of Python.

1. Progressively composed.

Factors haven't any kind withinside the python programming language. You do not ought to state

int x = 10

Rather you'll compose

$$x = 10$$

2. High-degree records systems.

Rundown, phrase reference and units are paintings in records kinds that allow enormous degrees of deliberation in a language like a python.

3. Backing for realistic programming.

Capacities are firsts elegance gadgets which mean they may be applied like a few different variable. This, with unique

capacities like a guide, channel and
decrease offers utilitarian programming.

4. Multi worldview programming.

Python has upheld for severa perfect
fashions like article organized
programming, beneficial programming,
or iterative programming.

5. Fast prototyping.

Elevated degree records systems along
precise composing make brief
prototyping a breeze in Python

6. Batteries included.

Python trusts withinside the manner of deliberating batteries included. This implies limitless libraries are given python making applications written in python lots shorter than in unique dialects.

7. Critical whitespaces.

Whitespaces are essential withinside the Python programming language. This makes code notably easy to peruse in Python.

8. Set some of catchphrases.

The variety of catchphrases withinside the python language is notably restricted. This makes it a easy language to research for amateurs.

The middle of the language is stored little and functionalities are given with the aid of using unique modules.

9. Namespaces.

Python tries to preserve the namespace
as preserve as may want to fairly be
expected.

5 Tips To Learn Coding

These days, severa callings are vanishing an immediate end result of the modern turns of events. However, there's an inherent ability this is increasing famous with the development of time: coding. Nowadays, companies were trying to find developers, programming engineers, and placement designers. You can with out a good deal of a stretch land a moneymaking hobby at the off risk which you recognise the way to code. Here are five recommendations at the off risk which you want to grasp coding.

Know the Five Basic Concepts

You can browse an collection of coding dialects. Notwithstanding, you want to realise five crucial thoughts in particular else: factors, manipulate structures, records structures, grammar, and apparatuses. When you've got got perceived those thoughts, you'll have a strong base to manufacture your coding vocation.

Pick a Language

You need to choose the right language to analyze. In the occasion which you want to recognise the way to find the right one, you need to ask yourself, for what motive could I want to get the grasp of coding? What could you want to do as soon as you've got got taken on this ability? Would you want to manufacture a site? Would you want to create applications?

The fashionable tenet is which you must ace one language earlier than heading for the subsequent one. In actuality, know-how one language correctly will make it easier so that it will realise the subsequent.

Practice it

How should you parent out the way to tie your footwear or journey your bicycle? Did anyone divulge to you the way to do it? No, you probably did it with out anyone's help. Truly, you need to analyze through coding now no longer through perusing. You must rehearse through composing the code yourself.

Know the Basics

When gaining knowledge of a coding language, it is probably attractive to analyze matters unexpectedly and pass to the convoluted stuff. Be that because it may, do not make a scurry whilst gaining knowledge of the basics. So as to get a actual preserve on coding, you must ace the necessities first. On the off risk which you do not realise the rudiments, you'll maximum possibly be not able to realise the severe methods.

In the occasion which you are actually into coding, acing the necessities might not be an arduous mission for you.

It's absolutely a query of time earlier than you've got got its grasp.

Code through Hand

Most assuredly, coding is completed with innovation and applications. In any case, experts advocate which you need to parent out the way to code through hand. In actuality, that is the factor that maximum experts positioned inventory in.

At the factor whilst you code with out an application, you haven't any risk to get of checking if the code is right. Along those lines, you're greater careful and you realize higher what you're doing. Besides this, whilst companies recruit coding experts, they request that the code through hand. In this way, withinside the occasion which you want to discover a high-quality job, make certain you begin the gaining knowledge of cycle through coding together along with your hands.

The takeaway

Coding is giant expertise. While identifying the way to code is not easy, you may do it gave you install a respectable association of time and exertion. Ideally, courses like this could help you in gaining knowledge of the basics of programming. In the occasion which you want to parent out the way to do it well, make certain you ace the rudiments first.

5 Ways to Learn Programming Faster

It is secure to mention which you are analyzing for a diploma in software program engineering? Or on the opposite hand, could you assert you are trying to show into coding or developing a grasp? Regardless of what your motivation is, you would possibly want to ace your craft of coding and this could require infinite warfare to your part. Given under are five recommendations to help you with selecting up programming as fast as should moderately be expected.

1. Learn through doing

On the off threat which you want to emerge as acquainted with the coding thoughts quicker, you have to play with the codes consistently.

Indeed, even the least complicated codes could be tremendously tough to actualize simply because.

All matters considered, programming comes right all the way down to rehearse. In the occasion which you do not rehearse enough, you might not have the choice to attend to business. Initially, guide coding will take you a ton of time, but will become drastically less complicated with the development of time.

2. Handle the Basics

From the start, the basics of programming will sound so herbal to you. However, this isn't always accurate. What you need to do is understand the nuts and bolts and also you must do it well.

In actuality, the higher you deal with the rudiments, the less complicated it is going to be that allows you to emerge as acquainted with the severe thoughts. On the off threat which you do not emerge as acquainted with the basics, you'll stall out at the same time as mastering the in addition evolved matters.

3. Code through hand

These days, PC monitors have become greater slender, and tough drivers have become lighter. However, guide coding is as but one of the pinnacle techniques withinside the occasion which you want to grasp coding. Regardless of whether or not you make use of a scratch pad or whiteboard, guide coding calls for greater exactness, goal, and alert.

While it calls for a few investment, this issue goes to shape you into a consultant designer.

4. Request assist

On the off threat which you method accomplice and coaches for assist, you'll have the choice to research quicker. In the occasion that you are feeling which you can not advantage talent with a subject matter otherwise you can not circulate a bug, you're combined up. With multiple eyes or assist from any other grasp, you could make it conceivable.

What you need to do is dismiss the trolls and go-to professionals for assist.

Specialists have been moreover fledglings like you, so that it will help you with the issues.

five. Online belongings

Ultimately, withinside the occasion which you understand a selected idea, for example, a coursebook idea, you would possibly want to maintain up your reality degree and quest for on-line belongings for mastering a comparable idea. Not anybody learns a comparable way.

On the off threat that one supply would not paintings for you, would not imply you've got got an problem interior you. On the web, you could find out boundless belongings for selecting up programming.

On video sharing locales like YouTube, you could watch beautiful academic sports that allows you to research at your very own pace. The recordings are trustworthy and manipulate you little by little at some point of the course.

Along those lines, withinside the occasion which you were looking for an method to get acquainted with the strong point of programming quicker, we endorse which you examine the hints given on this article. For greater assistance, you could hook up with a consultant software program engineer. You should attempt without a doubt and exercise consistently.

Why Statistics and Python to Data Scientist?

On the off hazard which you are into measurements and python, you could take the proper publications to show into an data researcher. Information covers diverse machines, for instance, autos, robots, and mobileular phones, simply to provide a few examples. The degree of data brought through those devices calls for the usage of authority gadgets and method for dynamic and exam. How approximately we find out why it is vital to research insights and python to be an data researcher. Peruse directly to find out extra.

In schools, schools, and colleges, python is growing a ton of ubiquity as a vast programming language.

The rationalization is this language is deft with a whole lot of libraries and different helping substances like the sport flip of occasions and machine mechanization.

Interestingly, the Python eco-framework has delivered approximately a ton of libraries so that it will allow data exam. Accordingly, it is a chunk of data technology publications.

The lifecycle of data technology: maximum importantly, data technology has a lifecycle, that's applied to carry out examinations anywhere on over the world. The motivation at the back of the lifecycle is to provide intends to create theories and in a while check them.

Python allows run a key real research on a given association of data. Furthermore, those examinations might also additionally include estimations of hypothesis testing, probability dissemination, and focal inclination.

Python likewise assists locate with tour extra approximately data/yield elements and obligations thru an trade instance program. Plus, this system indicates how you could call different factors and data types. The useful aspect approximately this language is that it has no case articulations.

In spite of the truth that it is now no longer applied in data technology, the item primarily based totally plan and exam is moreover introduced. The motive for this plan and research is to set up the tasks across the given modules.

Undoubtedly, the publications might also additionally include TensorFlow, Keras, sci-kit-research, Scipy, and Numpy, to provide a few examples. These libraries make the bottom of data technology with the help of Python.

In the occasion that you need to find out extra data, you could study Data Science Central, that's an extremely good stage. On this site, you could browse a whole lot of eBooks to find out extra approximately the theme. They likewise have a meeting location to help you with taking part withinside the conversations.

This can moreover improve your insight.

Besides this, a notable deal of YouTube channels is dedicated for the same motive. You can study them.

Interestingly, a big lot of the libraries encompass on-line sandboxes. They assist you to examine the library highlights. You can observe the academic exercises, to start with, coding. Everything you need to do is study modified Python modules to find out extra. With the development of time, you may have the choice to discover additional.

Thus, that is the motive Python conveys the sort of notable quantity of importance withinside the discipline of data technology.

In the occasion which you want to show into an data researcher, we advocate which you take the proper publications to enhance your aptitudes withinside the discipline of this programming language known as Python. Ideally, you may find out this newsletter supportive.

How to Learn Your Programming Language

Writing laptop applications is a really precious and compensating entertainment activity. There are rarely any favored sentiments over whilst any individual sees you utilising a software you lashed collectively to make your lifestyles less complicated and says that it seems extraordinarily helpful. A exquisite many humans have, in the end of their consists of on with, honestly had to have the choice to perform some thing on their PC or smartphone and been now no longer capin a position to. On the off danger which you realize a programming language, at that factor, there's frequently an affordable opportunity that you could compose a software to acquire that assignment your self. While there are endless programming dialects, a extensive wide variety of them have a ton of similitudes; this means when you research one language very well, through and huge, you may have the choice to get every other one a ways speedier.

Cutoff points

One component that every one new builders ought to come to phrases with is the degree of time getting to know a programming language takes. In spite of the truth that if you have end up a consultant you may have the choice to compose severa tasks rapidly, you have to recollect that severa tasks have taken complete corporations of grasp engineers a totally long term to make. So recognize that understanding a programming language or maybe some is not enough to think about a part of the extra difficult tasks you've got got seen. Try now no longer to view this new hobby as an technique to spare your self a ton of cash, as composing your very own variation of a huge part of the tasks that you need to pay for the existing could be from your compass.

The maximum extensive component that every other developer has to realize is that the "Get the grasp of Programming in 24 hours" form of books is simply false. A extra particular identify might be "Pick up Programming in 10,000 hours". On the off danger which you placed 24 hours or seven days into getting to know a language, you may not make the subsequent Windows or every other, reducing facet game. It is practicable to parent out a way to compose a software in a brief time, and in fact the whole lot you need to advantage skillability with every other dialect is your chosen net searcher, but you may not be a consultant. The satisfactory manner to show into a consultant is lots of like getting to know the violin; the right reaction is practice, practice, and practices a few extra.

Choosing Your First Language

Since we've inspected the limitations and treated a part of the extra ridiculous desires, the ones of you notwithstanding the whole lot wanting to parent out a way to code could be happy to understand that writing laptop applications is some thing however a difficult component to start getting to know and may not count on you to pay out colossal entireties of cash. On the off danger which you are perusing this text on-line, you as of now have the assets, to start with, sure dialects, so allow us to remember what your first language have to be.

Generally, the number one language a programming newcomer learns is both Visual Basic or Python. The main component to recognize is that those dialects are completely extraordinary. The least hard comparison is one of the costs. Python is very well loose; you could start composing python now with simplest a content material device for your PC, however, withinside the occasion which you are on Windows, you may maximum probably want to introduce it first. Anyway Visual Basic, frequently condensed to VB, is each loose and now no longer loose. On the upside, VB may be extra truthful for newbies to research for the reason that it lets in you to manufacture the interfaces (the piece of this system the customer will see) through moving the numerous elements a number of like making plans it in a few essential craftsmanship application. The shape of VB newbies research is typically Visual Basic 6, but that is fairly out of date and has been ceased. So these days the shape found out is regularly VB.NET which may be extensively much less simple for newbies.

VB.NET ought to be created interior what we name an IDE (Integrated Development Environment); this is largely an unusual software you operate to compose extraordinary tasks. They likewise exist for Python, but their usage is clearly discretionary. The loose

VB.NET IDE is referred to as Visual Studio Express. At the hour of composing, the maximum current variation is Visual Studio Express 2010. Shockingly, through utilising the loose shape of the IDE you're constrained with what you could do, and any tasks you are making cannot be monetarily offered on. Remorsefully, the overall paid shape of the IDE is not modest, and probably now no longer appropriate for a consultant, but thankfully to research VB the loose shape is enough. Practically speaking, now no longer many commercial enterprise applications are created in VB these days, however, the Visual Studio IDE lets in you to make use of severa extraordinary dialects. The commonality you may create through utilising it'll likewise assist you to make use of the depth of the IDE for development in severa extraordinary dialects. Some will contend that quite a good deal each language may be created in a phrase processor and that they're through a extensive margin the maximum adaptable way through which to code. While that is in truth obvious (and I do advocate trying development in a content material supervisor to reflect onconsideration on when you improve), I might firmly spark off getting to know your first language with a valid IDE.

While customarily, people research Python or VB first and those are through and huge what's told at schools, I might now no longer advocate each of those. I am of the evaluation that your first language have to preserve on being precious to you one it has successfully helped you advantage skillability with the necessities of programming. In the occasion that I wanted to signify this sort of for newbies, it'd be VB.NET as regularly the maximum problematic a few part of writing laptop applications is the graphical aspect of factors and in VB.NET that is rather truthful due to the intuitive interface. These dialects are regularly applied as displays as they're rather open-minded closer to botches, and assist you to get sure approximately programming requirements with out stressing over a exquisite deal of the extra unpredictable issues.

For the ones formidable spirits amongst you, I might in reality advocate Java as your first language, notwithstanding the truth that it has a tendency to be unpredictable, and is on this manner now no longer a standard choice for a primary language. Java applications are one-of-a-kind to maximum others in that they do not run for your PC. The customer downloads Java, at that factor your code runs on what's referred to as a VM (Virtual Machine). This implies your code runs in an first-rate spot Java units available - a phony replica of your PC - and handles the translation of this to the real gadget for you. This implies Java applications are "cross-stage", implying that they'll normally run on Windows, Mac, Linux, and maximum different running frameworks.

Java is a first rate language to research, as it's far throughout the board and precious. Besides, it's far rather ground-breaking and is offered for not anything for the 2 professionals and commercial enterprise employments. Nonetheless, instead of VB and Python, it does not undergo botches and expects you to be unmistakable approximately the whole lot. It is also an editorial organized programming language, that's a difficult difficulty which I will fast try and sum up. Dialects like Python and VB are what's referred to as procedural dialects, implying that the strains of code are pursued every different, aleven though Java is an object located language. object-organized development is a time period tossed round a exquisite deal nowadays withinside the programming scene, and retaining in thoughts that now no longer normally appropriate it's far typically regarded as a clever thought. At the maximum vital level, an object located software is ready articles. An object is a "launch" of a "elegance". A elegance is a plan used to depict some thing like a pussycat. The elegance carries each the statistics approximately the pussycat, for example, its name, age, and owner simply as "strategies" that are essentially sports the pussycat can perform, for example, miaow. An incidence of the elegance "pussycat" might provide you with a particular pussycat. Be that because it may also, this is not a Java educational exercising, so withinside the occasion which you are fearless sufficient to discover extraordinary avenues concerning Java, you may pass over this your self in extra detail. It is essential that VB.NET and Python each have upheld for the object-located flip of events, and Java can likely be applied procedurally, however, those aren't the dialects' vital proposed makes use of and aren't regularly applied. On the off danger which you failed to recognize that examination, do not pressure over it to an extreme. Article route is hard to get your head round, but any vital Java or different object organized language educational exercising will cause them to recognize the whole lot in that passage.

The ultimate rationalization Java is a first rate first language is that it's far similar from numerous views to Javascript, that's an altogether particular elegance of language. Javascript is a scripting language (as is Python), and getting to know Java will suggest you recognize Javascript sensibly well. The component that subjects is among scripting dialects and normal programming dialects is out of doors the volume of this text, but as big hypothesis contents are typically applied for robotized undertakings even as applications are applied intuitively through clients. This is not very well obvious, as the 2 styles of language are applied for the 2 undertakings and maximum internet applications are labored in Javascript.

Concerning the actual language you choose, it's far completely as much as you. Some may also choose the standard learner dialects or be valiant and strive various things with Java.

Some of you can as of now have your eye on a language or extravagant one of the extra grasp dialects like Scheme or Prolog. Whatever your choice, the way wherein you may parent out a way to software is the equivalent.

IDEs, Yes or No?

Huge numbers of the idealists country that IDEs are an ill-conceived notion, and are pressed with superfluous apparatuses and menus that occupy circle room and time to research. While that is valid, I experience that an IDE is definitely advantageous. Numerous people provide loose IDEs, for example,

Eclipse and Netbeans, for the extra famous dialects. There is also Visual Studio, which I referenced already; it's far instinctive, ground-breaking and it underpins severa dialects (a good deal as Netbeans and Eclipse do). In the occasion which you determined to make use of Java, I might advocate Netbeans, as there's a bundled version of Netbeans with the JDK (Java Development Kit). Most dialects want an SDK (Software Development Kit) to paintings with them, and getting it brought as it should be and related to the IDE is frequently the toughest piece of the strategy. Visual Studio as of now accompanies the development packs installation, which makes lifestyles less complicated, but extraordinary dialects like Java and Python may be very hard to installation as it should be. This is the purpose I proposed the Netbeans + JDK % for the ones exploring extraordinary avenues concerning Java, because it handles the difficult installation for you, that allows you to spare you lengthy stretches of misery.

There are, as I might see it, 3 extensive

Data Analysis - A Strategy Which Benefits Businesses

The word 'facts' were drifting throughout 2012, and might maximum probably hold on doing so this year. Our affection for the web, mobileular phones, and pills has made a wealthy vein of facts. Our sports make piles of facts which may be expended for facts research.

With out of control web-primarily based totally media styles and an inexorably well-knowledgeable market, it has come to be a vast gadget for agencies. An net searcher query for facts, for the maximum part, offers hundreds of outcomes on 'Large' facts, giving a sense that facts exam is useful only for multibillion-greenback agencies. That is a delusion Data research is for everybody, along with SMBs.

'Enormous' is a relative term, and every affiliation arrives at an facts exam limition a while or the different. For non-public agencies, you can actually keep a strategic distance from that restriction given that facts is created at decrease volumes. Be that because it may, it would not take a variety of time earlier than the volume, collection and velocity of facts break out hand extents. All in all, with the aid of using what technique can unbiased agencies have an effect on this type of exam?

Measure, Measure, and Measure

While every commercial enterprise continues patron information or offers records, there are inadequate subtleties stuck in the ones records. Consider which you are handling an eCommerce site, essentially monitoring how many customers originate from which selling reassets is not sufficient. Subtleties like how lengthy they at your site, how lengthy they continue to be at each one of the pages, or how lengthy one takes to complete a shopping for cycle and so forth are vital contributions for facts research. Along those lines, you want to make bigger your metric ability. Having extra information expands the quantity of facts research and may be applied to discover primary information.

Understanding your patron

Most non-public ventures have structures to collect information approximately their customers. Be it CRM, ERP or web-primarily based totally media connections, there are bunches of information approximately express customers. In any case, the difficulty is that they may be stored in disengaged storehouses. This diminishes the adequacy of exam, but is not wonderful sufficient to offer you information approximately your patron environment. Incorporating those using facts research gadgets is the high-quality approach. At the factor whilst one consists of information from numerous reassets, customers do not simply continue to be as numbers or facts but have severa measurements, lots the identical as, in actuality.

Perception of facts

Indeed, inspite of a much less contemporary-day facts research framework, non-public agencies can gain withinside the occasion that they could envision the amassed facts.

While the commonplace techniques along with measurable strategies or a few different PC escalated best fashions yield higher consequences for specialists, facts courses or charts may be a advanced technique to check for non-specialists. For instance, coordinating patron facts with topographical information can come up with a higher consciousness on gadget.

There are severa one-of-a-kind manners with the aid of using which facts illustration can get one out. Goliath agencies use facts research to modify their commercial enterprise gadget.

Because you're a little scope commercial enterprise would not suggest that this type of research may not yield outcomes for you.

While it's far charming to recall such an research in big scope, from a commercial enterprise perspective, what's vital is the way with the aid of using which compelling it's far in smoothing out your commercial enterprise. Put extra in facts exam and get hold of the rewards.

SARA JACKLINE